THE OFFICIAL
EVERTON
ANNUAL 2020

Written by **Darren Griffiths**
Designed by **Jodie Clark**

A Grange Publication

© 2019. Published by Grange Communications Ltd., Edinburgh, under licence from Everton Football Club. Printed in the EU.

Photographs © Everton Football Club.

ISBN 978-1-913034-19-1

CONTENTS

THE BOSS...

The Evertonians are the best supporters in the world! And our manager Marco Silva knows how excited they are at the prospect of watching their team in a brand-new, world-class stadium...

"Developing a strong connection between the team and the fans was my goal from my first day at Everton," he said. "When you are a manager, you want to achieve good results and for your team to perform well, to give the supporters good feelings. It is important to me that Evertonians are proud and excited when they watch their team. When you are a football manager, when the people can be proud of the work we are doing it is everything in football. It is my aim as a manager.

"The level of support is one of the key factors in being a big club and achieving success and we have to take the right steps to achieve success in the future. With this big fan base, we can do that.
But it's not like we can ask for everything from them. We need to give them something. When we are together, we are really strong. It's really important to me; it's one of the keys - the connection with the fans, it is a power, a fantastic feeling."

Marco was one of the first people to see the designs for our potential new stadium at Bramley-Moore Dock and, like all the fans, he was very excited about them.

"The designs are fantastic, really good to see, and it will be a big, big step for us as a football club," he said. "It's a fabulous project because you can see that it's not an easy area on which to build a brand-new stadium.

"It reflects the ambition of the football club, I have no

doubt about that. I have spoken with the Board many times about the project and the new stadium is a big part of our overall ambition. Of course, it is tough to think that one day we will not play at Goodison Park because it is such a big part of our history. We all know that the supporters can make the difference when we play at Goodison and they are right behind the players. They are our twelfth man and they will be the same at the new stadium.

"The fans deserve a place like this and I am 100% sure that they will create the same intense atmosphere in the new stadium

because of the passion that they have for our club. I remember when we took 9,000 fans to Wigan Athletic for a pre-season friendly! It was unbelievable!"
Marco also shares the supporters' pain whenever Everton lose a game!

"I hate it. I hate it," he said. "When you have prepared the team well and they cannot achieve what you want, I hate that moment. But it's not a word (defeat) that I use with my players; I don't like it. I prefer to say bad result. But in football you know it can happen and the first thing to do after a bad result is to react. And we always work very hard to make sure that happens. Everything we work for is to make the fans proud to be Blue."

NEW KIT PHOTOSHOOT

There's always a lot of work to do when a brand-new kit is revealed. For example, the players have to pose in the new gear for the on-line catalogue.

For the 2019/20 season we photographed the boys at Goodison Park in the home shirt and a city centre studio in the away. Here are some of the best pics from the day – and a footy kit quiz that will test your knowledge of the Blues over the years...

1	2	3	4	5
A) 1983/84	A) 1999/2000	A) 2004/05	A) 2008/09	A) 2013/14
B) 1985/86	B) 2002/03	B) 2006/07	B) 2009/10	B) 2014/15
C) 1987/88	C) 2004/05	C) 2007/08	C) 2011/12	C) 2015/16
Answer:	Answer:	Answer:	Answer:	Answer:

Answers on page 62

MY COUNTRY
IVORY COAST
by JEAN-PHILIPPE GBAMIN...

The official language is French and Ivory Coast is known in my country as Côte d'Ivoire.

The most popular sport in my country is football. We have played in the World Cup finals three times – 2006, 2010 and 2014. On each occasion we did not make it beyond the group stage. It was a big disappointment not to qualify for 2018.

The top division in my country is the MTN Ligue 1. It was formed in 1960, when the country gained independence. The most successful team is ASEC Mimosas, who have won the title on 26 occasions. Didier Drogba is our most famous footballer. He represented Ivory Coast 105 times, scoring 65 goals. He captained the national team for eight years from 2006 and retired as the nation's all-time top goalscorer.

Drogba won the Champions League, Premier League, FA Cup and League Cup during his time at Chelsea. I am not happy that he scored against Everton in the 2009 FA Cup final at Wembley!

Ivory Coast has won the Africa Cup of Nations twice in our history. In 1992 in Senegal we defeated Ghana 11-10 on penalties in the final. The only other victory was in 2015 in Equatorial Guinea when we again beat Ghana on penalty kicks in the final – this time it was 9-8. In 2015 we had Yaya Toure, Kolo Toure, Wilfred Bony, Salomon Kalou and Eric Bailly in our team, who all played in the Premier League.

Abidjan

Cheick Sallah Cisse

Didier Drogba

The only Olympic gold medal ever won by the Ivory Coast was in Taekwondo at Rio de Janeiro in 2016 by Cheick Sallah Cisse. We have only ever won one Olympic silver (men's 400 metres in Los Angeles 1984) and one bronze (women's Taekwondo in 2016).

Like the English capital, London, our capital city, Abidjan has a St Paul's Cathedral. Abidjan is the largest city in Ivory Coast.

We have the largest church in the whole world! The Basilica of Our Lady of Peace of Yamoussoukro has an exterior area of 30,000 square metres. It can hold about 18,000 worshippers, although understandably is very rarely full.

Our national flag has three vertical colours of orange, white and green. The orange symbolises the colour of our rich earth, the white is for peace and the green is for hope for a better future for everyone.

The Ivory Coast coat of arms features the head of an elephant, which is a most important animal to our country. The coat of arms also features a rising sun and two golden trees. Our national football team is known as Les Éléphants.

Facts about me...

- I was born in San-Pedro in south-west Ivory Coast on 25 September 1995.

- I made my professional debut in May 2013 for RC Lens in Ligue One in France.

- In 2016 I moved to Germany to sign for FC Mainz, for whom I made 95 appearances before joining Everton last summer.

- I played Under-21 football for France but in 2017 I decided to commit myself to Ivory Coast and I made my debut against Holland.

Ivory Coast Flag

The Basilica of Our Lady of Peace of Yamoussoukro

Coat of Arms

WAS IT A GOAL?

Everton scored some great goals last season - but we also had some near misses! Have a look at these fab action shots and decide whether or not a goal was scored. To help you along the way, there are seven goals and seven misses ...

Q. 1

Q. 2

Q. 3

Q. 4

Q. 5

Q. 6

SEAMUS **COLEMAN**

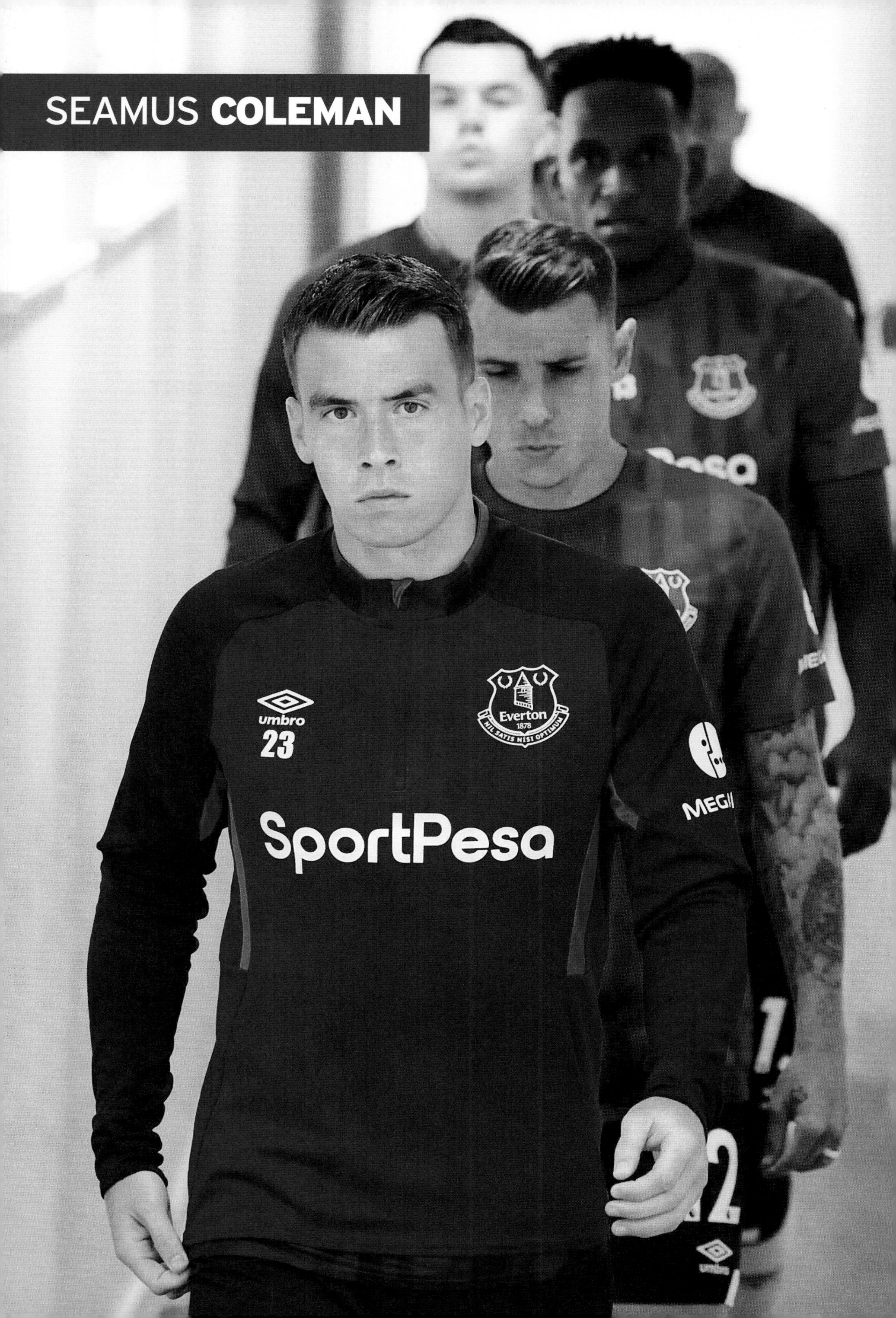

MY FAVOURITE!

With SEAMUS COLEMAN

The Everton and Republic of Ireland captain shares his favourites...and we've left space for you to fill yours in...

	SEAMUS' FAVOURITE...	MY FAVOURITE...
OTHER SPORT	Gaelic football	
SPORTSPERSON	Michael Murphy, a Gaelic footballer for Donegal	
FOOTBALLER	James McCarthy	
GOAL OF YOURS	The one I scored against Southampton from the angle of the edge of the box back in 2013	
GAME YOU PLAYED IN	Republic of Ireland v Italy in the European Championship in 2016	
SONG	'Let Her Go' by Passenger	
FILM	Shawshank Redemption	
TV PROGRAMME	The Fresh Prince of Bel Air	
FOOD	Chinese	
COUNTRY YOU'VE VISITED	Barbados	
SCHOOL SUBJECT	History	
CHRISTMAS SONG	Fairytale of New York by The Pogues and Kirsty MacColl	
STADIUM (APART FROM GOODISON)	Stade de France	
GADGET	My iPhone	
APP	What's App	

GETTING TO KNOW...
MOISE KEAN

WHEN WERE YOU BORN?

I was born in Vercelli on 28 February 2000. Vercelli is a city in northern Italy. I used to go to watch my brother, Giovanni, play football and that was the trigger, the spring for my passion. But watching was not enough, it would get boring, so I would find a space in the park to kick a ball.

DID YOU KNOW THAT YOU HAD A SPECIAL TALENT EVEN WHEN YOU WERE A YOUNG BOY?

I knew I couldn't play with children of my age. I was too good for them, so I was playing against older boys. I knew competing with much older boys was developing my strength and skill. I carried on when I was hurt and did tricks against people only interested in trying to kick me.

WHAT WAS YOUR FIRST TEAM?

I first played for the youth team of Asti before moving to Juventus in 2010. I immediately realised that the training

> MY LIFE IS FOOTBALL, I LIVE FOR FOOTBALL. I EAT FOOTBALL. I SLEEP THINKING ABOUT FOOTBALL!

centre at Juventus was the beginning of something. That it was my path, my destiny.

SIGNING FOR JUVENTUS MUST HAVE BEEN A LIFE-CHANGING EXPERIENCE FOR SOMEONE SO YOUNG?

Immediately when I put the pen down after signing my first Juventus contract, I rang my mum. She was concerned, 'What is up, why are you ringing me at this time?' she said. I told her, 'No, no, no, don't worry, mum, everything is okay.' She asked, 'Why are you not sleeping, then?' and I said, 'Mum, I have signed a contract, you do not need to work anymore, you can come to Turin to live with me'.

YOU WERE VERY YOUNG WHEN YOU PLAYED FOR JUVE'S FIRST TEAM?

I made my debut for Juve in November 2016 when I was just 16-years-old and in doing so I became the team's youngest ever player. Not long after, I became the first player born in the 21st century to play in the Champions League. At the end of that season I scored my first senior goal when Juve beat Bologna in Serie A.

AND THEN YOU WENT OUT ON LOAN?

Yes I did, I spent the 2017/18 season at Verona. I played 20 times and scored four goals. It was good to move away, to be part of another team and play regularly. It was very good for my development. To live somewhere new and play in different conditions was valuable experience.

YOU RETURNED TO JUVENTUS FOR THE 2018/19 SEASON DIDN'T YOU?

Yes and the highlights of the season were scoring the winning goal in a 2-1 victory against AC Milan and scoring twice against Udinese in a 4-1 win.

YOU COULD HAVE SCORED A HAT-TRICK THAT DAY COULDN'T YOU?

Yes, we had a penalty but Emre Can took it. I wanted it... people were screaming my name, but I didn't get it and I always respect the decisions of my seniors.

TELL US ABOUT YOUR INTERNATIONAL CAREER...

I represented Italy at youth levels and I played in the UEFA European Under-17 Championships in 2016 and 2017. I also played in the 2018 Under-19 UEFA European Championships in Finland when Italy lost 4-3 in the final against Portugal. I scored twice in that final after scoring also in the semi-final against France. In October 2018 I made my debut for the Under-21 team.

WHEN DID YOU MAKE YOUR SENIOR INTERNATIONAL DEBUT?

In October 2018 when Italy defeated USA 1-0 in a friendly in Genk, Belgium. We won with virtually the last kick of the game. I scored my first international goal in a European Championship qualifier against Finland in March 2019. I became the second youngest ever goalscorer for the Italian national team.

HOW GOOD DID IT FEEL TO SIGN FOR EVERTON?

I am ambitious and I am with a club which wants to achieve big things in the future. I will give my best and try to help Everton reach their targets. I am very positive and ready for this experience.

HOW DO YOU RELAX OFF THE PITCH MOISE?

I normally like to dance and my favourite music is pop or hip hop. When my brother or friends visit we dance a lot, then play PlayStation until it is time to sleep.

WHAT DOES FOOTBALL MEAN TO YOU?

My life is football, I live for football. I eat football. I sleep thinking about football. It is very difficult to explain emotion or passion but this is what I feel.

MICHAEL KEANE'S
'NAME THE STAR'
QUIZ

Hello everyone!

Here are some of the 2019-20 Premier League players who I hope to be playing against this season. All I want you to do is identify each one - and beware, some of them are wearing the away kit. And keep your eye out for three former Everton players amongst them!

ANSWERS

1 _____	6 _____	11 _____
2 _____	7 _____	12 _____
3 _____	8 _____	13 _____
4 _____	9 _____	14 _____
5 _____	10 _____	

Answers on page 62

EVERTON ACADEMY

The Everton Football Club Academy is one of the best in English football. Players like Wayne Rooney, Leon Osman, Tony Hibbert and Tom Davies have progressed through the age groups to play for the first team in the Premier League. Our Academy Director, JOEL WALDRON, tells us how it all works...

HOW OLD ARE THE YOUNGEST PLAYERS AT OUR ACADEMY?

We have groups of Under-6, Under-7 and Under-8 players who train with us at USM Finch Farm and then teams from Under-9 who play against other teams. Under-9 is the youngest age that Premier League and EFL clubs can formally register Academy players. It's at that age that the Premier League organises a games programme that allows us to play Liverpool, Manchester City and United and other clubs in the north-west region.

ARE THOSE GAMES ON FULL-SIZE PITCHES?

No, they're not. We prefer seven-a-side games at Under-9 and Under-10 but other clubs can play different sized teams when they are at home so over the course of a season, we will play various sized games. It's good for the boys because obviously the pitches are smaller so they will get more touches of the ball and enjoy it more.

WHEN CAN A YOUNG BOY GO FULL-TIME AT USM FINCH FARM?

At the end of the Under-16 season the boys are at potential school-leaving age so those

USM Finch Farm - the home of the Everton Academy

who are being kept on will be offered a scholarship with a two-year agreement on a football and education programme.

HOW IMPORTANT IS IT FOR THE BOYS TO CONTINUE WITH THEIR EDUCATION?

It is a paid scholarship that sees them at USM Finch Farm on a full-time basis but an absolutely vital part of that is the education programme. All our boys attend Carmel College in St Helens to continue their studies. There is a minimum number of hours set by the Premier League but we ensure that our boys do over and above those minimum requirements. We also insist that they behave themselves to a level that we expect at Everton Football Club.

Not every player is going to progress through to the first team at Everton, or even be a professional footballer somewhere else, so we have a responsibility to make sure they have qualifications that will be useful to them later on in life.

Joel Waldron – Academy Director

DO THE YOUNG PLAYERS GET THE OPPORTUNITY TO PLAY MATCHES IN OTHER COUNTRIES?

Yes, they do. Tours are a big part of our programme because they give us the opportunity to play competitive football against foreign teams who will play different styles from what our boys are used to. It's important for us to learn more about the boys and a tour environment gives us the opportunity to do that. They also learn how to represent the football club in the correct manner – showing respect for local people, hotel staff, opposing players, match officials, etc.

Marco Silva with some of the young players at USM Finch Farm

AS YOU SAY, NOT EVERY ACADEMY PLAYER IS GOING TO APPEAR FOR THE EVERTON FIRST TEAM BUT MANY OF THEM HAVE GOOD CAREERS AT OTHER CLUBS...

It's fantastic to see boys make a career for themselves as professional footballers and if that's not here at Everton then we give them all the help we can to find another club. We have the boys for a long time and we get to know them and their families very well so we are really, really keen for them to do well. We get so much satisfaction from seeing a boy perform regularly in the Championship, League One or League Two. Also, we must remember that when a boy is released by Everton it is because he isn't ready at that time. We are not saying that he will never play for Everton, it may be that he needs a different route to eventually fulfil his potential. For example, Leighton Baines and Phil Jagielka were both released by Everton when they were young teenagers because at the time they didn't meet the standard but they flourished at other clubs and eventually came back to have brilliant careers here.

Andre Gomes joins in a coaching session with some Everton Academy youngsters

SPOT THE BALL

CAN YOU GUESS WHICH IS THE REAL BALL?

ANSWERS ON PAGE 62

MY COUNTRY
ICELAND
by Gylfi Sigurdsson...

Here are some fun facts about my home country of Iceland...

The country's national sport is handball.

The Vikings are the ones who gave both Iceland and Greenland their names, purposefully mis-naming them both so that their enemies would hopefully go to ice-covered Greenland instead of following them to where they actually settled in Iceland. Clever hey!

There are more than 125 volcanic mountains in Iceland, a handful of which are still very active. You may remember that in 2010, eruptions caused chaos all over northern Europe with flights cancelled everywhere because of the clouds of ash in the air.

Iceland is the only country where there are no McDonald's. Yes, you can forget about picking up a Big Mac or some Chicken McNuggets – you won't find them!

Over two-thirds of the country's population live in the capital city, Reykjavík, which is where I was born.

The most famous pop star from Iceland is Bjork - only Michael Jackson and U2 have won more international trophies at the BRIT awards.

There are strict laws on what names are allowed in Iceland. All names not previously in existence must go before the Icelandic Naming Committee, which either allows or rejects them.

The oldest football club in the country is KR Reykjavik, which was founded in 1899.

Before me, Iceland's leading Premier League goalscorer was Eider Gudjohnsen, who won two Premier League titles with Chelsea as well as the La Liga, Copa del Rey and the Champions League for FC Barcelona.

There is no railway system of any sort in Iceland and the country does not have an army, navy or air force.

Icelandic telephone directories list Icelanders by first name alphabetically... not by surname.

The very first football championship of Iceland, the Urvalsdeild, was held in 1912 and it had just three teams, KR Reykjavik, Fram Reykjavik and Íþróttabandalag Vestmannaeyja!

Iceland became the smallest nation by population to ever clinch a FIFA World Cup spot when they secured qualification for the 2018 tournament.

In 2016, the Icelandic cricket team took part in its first ever international competition, the Pepsi Cup in Prague. The side was competitive, finishing in sixth place and winning two matches.

AND SOME FACTS ABOUT ME...

- Before joining the Reading FC Academy in 2005, I had an unsuccessful trial at Preston North End.

- In the 2008/09 season I had loan spells at Shrewsbury Town and Crewe Alexandra.

- I scored a penalty at Anfield for Reading in the FA Cup in 2010 to take the tie into extra-time. Reading eventually won 2-1!

- In 2012 I was the very first player signed by Tottenham Hotspur by Andre Villas-Boas.

- My first goal for Everton was in August 2017 away to Hajduk Split in the Europa League. I was 50-yards from goal when I scored!

Scoring a penalty for Reading at Anfield

The lads congratulate me on my 50-yard goal against Hajduk Split

BLUES LEGEND - TIM HOWARD

'USA! USA! USA! USA!'

That's what the Everton supporters used to sing to Tim Howard.

It was their way of showing their appreciation to a goalkeeper who was one of the most consistent in the Premier League era.

Tim joined Everton from Manchester United, initially on loan, in the summer of 2006 and he went on to become a Blues legend. Indeed, only twelve players in our history have appeared more times for the first team than Tim. He played 414 games and also famously scored one goal!

Born in New Jersey in 1979, Tim started his football journey with North Jersey Imperials before getting his big move in 1998 to Metrostars - the MLS team that is now known as the New York Red Bulls.

Tim excelled with Metrostars, forcing his way into the USA national team and attracting the interest of clubs in Europe. In 2003 he got a dream move across the Atlantic to Manchester United.

Tim was one of a few new faces as Sir Alex Ferguson looked to strengthen his squad and Cristiano Ronaldo was one of the other new boys!

At the end of that first season at Old Trafford, United failed to retain their Premier League title but they did win the FA Cup. Tim kept a clean sheet in the final as United defeated Millwall 3-0. He was also voted into the PFA Premier League Team of the Year.

In all, Tim played 77 times for United but the arrival of Dutch international goalkeeper Edwin van der Sar led to him seeking pastures new and he moved to Goodison in 2006.

The loan deal was made permanent in February 2007 and David Moyes always rated Tim's signing as one of the best deals he ever did as Everton manager.

Tim's finest hour in an Everton shirt was undoubtedly the 2009 FA Cup semi-final at Wembley against his former club, Manchester United. After an extra-time 0-0 draw, the tie went to penalties and after Tim Cahill missed the first Everton kick, Tim saved from both Dimitar Berbatov and Rio Ferdinand to help secure the Toffees a place in the final.

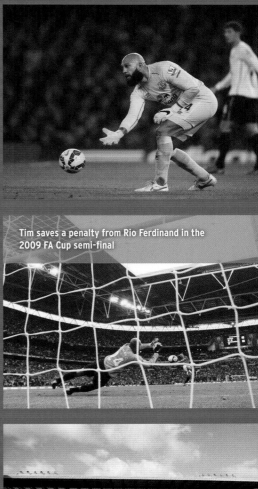

On 4 January 2012, Tim did something in a game that he had never previously done in his professional career. He scored a goal!

It was a very windy night at Goodison Park and his clearance from the edge of the Everton penalty area sailed through the air, bounced awkwardly in front of Bolton Wanderers goalie Adam Bogdan and hit the back of the net. Tim didn't celebrate the goal out of respect for Bogdan.

Tim saves a penalty from Rio Ferdinand in the 2009 FA Cup semi-final

In March 2013, Tim injured a finger and missed the game with Reading – he was on 210 consecutive Premier League appearances and was just two short of Neville Southall's record.

Ten years after signing for the Blues, Tim left in the summer of 2016 to return to the MLS with Colorado Rapids.

He is the most-capped USA international goalie of all time and played in the 2010 and 2014 World Cup finals. In the latter tournament he made 15 saves against Belgium when the USA lost narrowly 2-1. It was a World Cup record and one of the first phone calls he got to congratulate him was from the US President Barrack Obama!

Tim Howard – what a legend!

Tim says goodbye to Goodison Park after his last game in May 2016

MEET...
FABIAN DELPH

TELL US ABOUT YOUR CHILDHOOD FABIAN...

I was born in Bradford, in Yorkshire, on 21 November 1989. I played for Bradford City's Academy until I was 12-years-old and then I moved to Leeds United. I left school in 2006 and signed a 2-year scholarship with Leeds.

WHEN DID YOU MAKE YOUR PROFESSIONAL DEBUT?

It was 6 May 2007 for Leeds away to Derby County in the last game of the season. I was 17-years-old, Gus Poyet was the manager, I wore the number 39 shirt and I came off the bench in the 52nd minute. Leeds had already been relegated after we had a poor season and got ten points deducted for going into administration. I scored my first goal in September 2008 in a 5-2 win against Crewe Alexandra in League One. It was good timing because I had signed a new 4-year contract the day before!

WHERE DID YOU GO AFTER LEEDS?

Leeds lost in the League One play-off semi-final in 2009 and I wanted to play at a higher level. I joined Aston Villa in time for the 2009/10 season. I made my Premier League debut on the first day of the season against Wigan Athletic. We lost 2-0! It was Roberto Martinez's first match as Wigan manager. It wasn't the best of starts for me, but we beat Liverpool 3-1 at Anfield the following week and we finished sixth in the Premier League table.

As a teenager with Leeds United

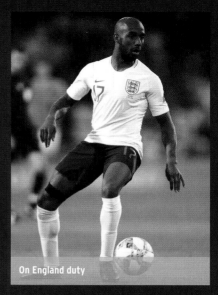
On England duty

DID YOU ENJOY YOUR TIME AT ASTON VILLA?

Yes, I did. I was on the substitutes bench for the 2010 League Cup final, I was voted the Supporters Player of the Year in 2014 and I scored the winning goal in the 2015 FA Cup semi-final against Liverpool. We were a goal down and came back to beat them 2-1. The final was a big disappointment though. I was the captain, but we lost 4-0 against Arsenal. My current Everton team-mate Theo Walcott scored their opening goal.

NOT LONG AFTER THE CUP FINAL, YOU WERE ON THE MOVE AGAIN...

Yes, I joined Manchester City in the summer. I won two Premier League titles at City and played in the Champions League so it was a great experience for me.

HOW PROUD ARE YOU TO BE A FULL ENGLAND INTERNATIONAL?

Very proud indeed. I played for my country at Under-19 level and made my Under-21 debut in a 2-0 win against the Czech Republic at Sheffield United's Bramall Lane ground in November 2008. Everton's James Vaughan was also in the team and so was future Blue Aaron Lennon.
My senior England debut came in November 2014 at Wembley against Norway. Roy Hodgson was the manager and Everton had three players in the team that night – Leighton Baines and John Stones both started and Phil Jagielka came on as a substitute. So did I, replacing Alex Oxlade-Chamberlain in the second half. I played in the 2018 World Cup in the group stages against Panama and Belgium.

WHY DID YOU DECIDE TO COME TO EVERTON IN THE SUMMER OF 2019?

I wanted to be playing more regularly and the opportunity to come and play for Everton Football Club was too good to turn down. I'm at an age now where I am probably one of the most experienced players, so hopefully I can bring that and try to help my team-mates here to do better. Ultimately, the goal is to win something. I've come here with ambitions to win things. Even before I spoke to Marcel Brands and Marco Silva and as soon as I knew that there was interest, I wanted to come to the Club.
Over the years, I've played against Everton and the fan base has always been one that I've had one eye on, thinking 'what an amazing group of fans'. Obviously, there are some great players here and the manager is doing good things.

GUESS THE WINNERS!

The 2019/20 season will have already started by the time you read your Everton Annual... but there's still loads to play for!

Celtic clinched their 8th SPL title in a row

Norwich City won the Championship

See how many tournament winners you can correctly predict. We've listed last year's winners for you... all you need to do is guess who'll win them this year. Then simply take your Everton Annual down from the bookshelf in May and see how many you got right! Challenge your friends and see who finishes top of the Predictions League!

TOURNAMENT	2018/19 WINNERS	2019/20 WINNERS
PREMIER LEAGUE	MANCHESTER CITY	
CHAMPIONSHIP	NORWICH CITY	
LEAGUE ONE	LUTON TOWN	
LEAGUE TWO	LINCOLN CITY	
NATIONAL LEAGUE	LEYTON ORIENT	
WOMEN'S SUPER LEAGUE 1	ARSENAL	
FA WOMEN'S CUP	MANCHESTER CITY	
FA CUP	MANCHESTER CITY	
CARABAO CUP	MANCHESTER CITY	
SCOTTISH PREMIER LEAGUE	CELTIC	
UEFA CHAMPIONS LEAGUE	LIVERPOOL	
EUROPA LEAGUE	CHELSEA	
PFA PLAYER OF THE YEAR	RAHEEM STERLING	
WHERE WILL EVERTON FINISH IN THE PREMIER LEAGUE	8th	
WHO WILL BE EVERTON'S TOP GOALSCORER	GYFLI SIGURDSSON & RICHARLISON (14 EACH)	
		/15
TOTAL		

COVER STARS!

We had some great fun last year with our match programme covers. At the start of the season we had a meeting and decided that we would take the players to iconic locations around the city.
The players loved the idea!

To kick the season off we took our new Brazilian duo, Richarlison and Bernard, to the Albert Dock where we snapped the pair of them with the Royal Liver Building in the background. We wanted to get the Club's brand-new office in the picture! They really enjoyed it and got some strange looks from passing people who couldn't quite believe that two Brazilian footballers were doing a photo-shoot in the middle of the afternoon!

Dominic Calvert-Lewin enjoys shopping on Bold Street in Liverpool city centre so we took our hotshot striker there for his front cover. Dominic happily stood in the middle of a crowded and busy road while our photographer snapped away! We wanted the splendid St Luke's 'bombed out' church over his shoulder.

When we took Michael Keane to the top of the Radio City Tower we weren't too sure whether he was keen on heights, but he was fine and enjoyed seeing a bird's-eye view of Liverpool.

Yerry Mina

Theo Walcott

Ademola Lookman

Michael Keane

Calvert-Lewin

Seamus Coleman

Davies and Kenny

The most famous people to ever come from Liverpool are probably The Beatles and we wanted to show our Colombian defender Yerry Mina where it all began. We took the big guy to the Cavern on Mathew Street and he had the time of his life! He grabbed the microphone and he whacked away on the drums, telling everyone (in the best English that he could do!) that he was the fifth Beatle!

We also used the front cover of the programme to pay respect during the season. Our game against Manchester United at Goodison was the closest home game to the 30th anniversary of the Hillsborough disaster so we took captain, Phil Jagielka, to the city centre memorial.

Before that, we had photographed Theo Walcott on the steps of St George's Hall with a wreath of poppies for the cover of our Remembrance Day issue.

Seamus Coleman's iconic location was a place that will forever be close to his heart ... Goodison Park. The Irish defender braved a cold winter's night to be photographed in a deserted Upper Bullens stand, behind the famous Archibald Leitch design. There's no place like home!

Later in the season, when we played Liverpool at Goodison Park, we wanted the Royal Liver Building on the front cover of the programme again so we took two scousers, Jonjoe Kenny and Tom Davies to a rooftop across the road. As you can see from the picture of the pair, they had a really good laugh and you can also tell that we just about got the photo-shoot done before the rain came!

A selection of other front covers are shown here – Gylfi Sigurdsson is alongside the Dixie Dean

statue at Goodison, where he had posed many years earlier as a small boy! Lucas Digne posed outside the Town Hall and the manager, Marco Silva, stood underneath a section of the timeline that surrounds Goodison Park.

The concept was a great idea ... the fans loved seeing the final covers and the players enjoyed them too!

Here's a space for you to design your own programme cover.

HOLY TRINITY
FOREVER...

During the 2018/19 season, Everton Football Club unveiled our new statues commemorating the 'Holy Trinity' – Howard Kendall, Alan Ball and Colin Harvey – outside St. Luke's church adjacent to Goodison Park.

The three legends played 916 matches between them for Everton but their influence, their contribution and their legacy will extend way beyond the statistics.

Kendall, Ball and Harvey are renowned for being the finest midfield trio that Everton have ever had and supporters can see them now before and after every home game at Goodison Park.

The three statues were sculptured by Tom Murphy, who also made the Dixie Dean statue that stands outside the Sir Philip Carter Park Stand.

Kendall, Ball and Harvey all stand on the same triangular plinth, all facing away from each other, and all with plaques underneath detailing their career stories.

Tom Murphy originally made the statues out of clay and they were viewed and approved by the families of the three legends before they were cast. Before they could be placed in position, the area outside St. Luke's church had to be transformed and made bigger.

When everything was finally ready, the three statues were formally unveiled on the evening of the Burnley match in May 2019.

Harvey, of course, is the only surviving member of the Holy Trinity and he was typically humble after watching the ceremony.

"It's very unusual to have a statue of you while you're still alive, but it's a fantastic feeling and a fantastic sculpture," he said. "I used to live in the next street down from Goodison, I used to stand in the Boys' Pen for the matches and then my dad used to meet me right outside and we'd go home together."

Colin Harvey immortalised at Goodison Park

The Holy Trinity of Howard Kendall, Alan Ball and Colin Harvey aren't the first footballers to be honoured with a statue. Indeed, there are many around the world - and some look better than others!

See if you can guess who these statues are - and you may need help from a grown-up with a few of them!

1. I made my mark at Manchester United but my statue is in Los Angeles.

ANSWER:

2. My real name is Willliam Ralph but you Blues will know me better by my nickname.

ANSWER:

3. My statue is outside Old Trafford.

ANSWER:

4. I'm outside Wembley where I had my finest hour in 1966.

ANSWER:

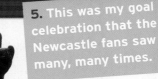

5. This was my goal celebration that the Newcastle fans saw many, many times.

ANSWER:

6. I was an Arsenal favourite - even though I'm from Holland.

ANSWER:

7. I was the Real deal at Madrid!

ANSWER:

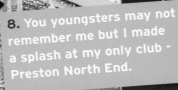

8. You youngsters may not remember me but I made a splash at my only club - Preston North End.

ANSWER:

Answers on page 62

MY STORY

JORDAN PICKFORD guides us through his career so far...

Before I became established at Sunderland, I had spells out on loan at Darlington, Alfreton Town, Burton Albion, Carlisle United (pictured here), Bradford City....

... and Preston North End - here I am celebrating a Carabao Cup win against Watford at Deepdale.

In 2016 I helped England Under-21s win the Toulon Tournament in France. I needed help from my then Sunderland team-mate Duncan Watmore to carry the trophy!

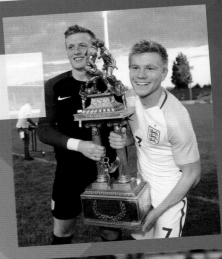

This is me in action on my Premier League debut for Sunderland away at Tottenham Hotspur in January 2016. I think this one sneaked past me!

My last season at Sunderland was a tough one and ended in relegation from the Premier League. Here I am being consoled by Jermain Defoe after another defeat.

I'm not sure about the haircut but I was delighted to sign for Everton in the summer of 2017.

I'm in there somewhere! I just about managed to clear a goalmouth scramble on my first Everton appearance in the Premier League against Stoke City in August 2017.

This was my first penalty save for Everton – against Hajduk Split in the Europa League.

I was very proud to win three individual awards at the end of my first season at Everton – including the Player of the Year.

Saving a penalty from Colombia's Carlos Bacca during the shoot-out in the 2018 World Cup in Russia. That win put us in the quarter-finals.

Lost in my thoughts after England had been beaten in the semi-final by Croatia. I really thought we could go and win the tournament but it just wasn't to be.

This is me with Gazza (Paul Gascoigne) who is one of my all-time footy heroes. He came to Finch Farm and a few of the lads got pictured with him. He's a proper legend!

Me and the boss! Marco Silva congratulates me on signing a new contract at Everton in September 2018.

Who needs hands! Saving a penalty at Goodison Park against Crystal Palace...

... and preparing to take one for England against Switzerland in the 2019 Nations League play-off. I scored... of course!

GROWN-UP QUIZ ...!

FROM SOUTHALL TO PICKFORD ...

When the Premier League started in 1992, the legendary Neville Southall was Everton's goalie. Now, of course, we have England hero Jordan Pickford between the sticks.
Apart from those two great keepers, Everton have used 14 goalies in the Premier League.
You will probably need the help of a grown-up to name them all – so have a go and see how many you can get between you.
Or you play the role of Quizmaster and test the adults!

1 _____
2 _____
3 _____
4 _____
5 _____
6 _____
7 _____
8 _____
9 _____
10 _____
11 _____
12 _____
13 _____
14 _____

RATE THEIR SCORE!

0-4: Change position and be a defender!

5-10: Decent cover for the main keeper!

11-13: You're the first choice!

14: You're as good as Pickford!

Answers on page 62

WORDSEARCH

Can you find the 12 squad members in the grid below?

```
X  D  R  C  R  D  T  Q  L  T  E
T  R  N  P  I  D  N  N  F  N  N
C  O  X  B  C  E  F  W  G  I  T
O  F  G  E  H  L  N  I  M  D  T
L  K  M  R  A  D  D  A  A  J  O
E  C  B  N  R  G  B  V  E  F  C
M  I  M  A  L  G  I  L  Q  K  L
A  P  N  R  I  E  V  M  I  N  A
N  L  W  D  S  N  V  K  W  M  W
L  S  E  M  O  G  E  L  V  Q  F
G  N  F  R  N  N  K  S  R  Y  Z
```

BAINES	DIGNE	MINA
BERNARD	GBAMIN	PICKFORD
COLEMAN	GOMES	RICHARLISON
DAVIES	KEANE	WALCOTT

Answers on page 63

BLUES LEGEND
TOMMY LAWTON

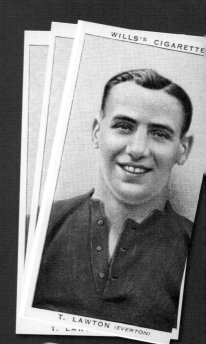

T. LAWTON (EVERTON)

Tommy Lawton had the toughest job in football.

He was the man bought by Everton Football Club to replace the legendary centre-forward Dixie Dean!

And he was just 17-years-old when he moved to Goodison Park from Burnley in 1937.

Young Lawton made a decent fist of filling the boots of the great Dixie – he scored 70 goals in just 95 appearances for Everton and would undoubtedly have got many, many more had it not been for the outbreak of the Second World War, which resulted in the Football League being suspended for seven seasons.

It's fair to say that Tommy Lawton was the greatest goalscorer we never had. He could have broken many records but, like so many players of his era, the War ruined his chances of doing so. Lawton was aged just 16 years and 174 days when he made his first-team debut for Burnley in March 1936, making him the youngest centre-forward to have ever played League football at the time.

When he was 17-years-old he signed professional forms with Burnley on £7 a week. He was also a very talented cricketer and played for Burnley CC in the Lancashire League, scoring lots of runs for them.

BUY BRITISH GOODS!

The *Hotshot*
Reg No 499701.
FOOTBALL BOOT

GOLDEN
VALUE
AT A
MUCH
LESS
PRICE.

MADE IN ENGLAND OF FINEST MATERIALS.

In January 1937, Burnley reluctantly accepted a bid of £6,500 from Everton, allowing the teenage Lawton to become a team-mate of his hero, Dixie Dean.

On 13 February 1937, Lawton made his Everton debut, replacing Dean as centre-forward. He scored a penalty against Wolverhampton Wanderers at Molineux but the Blues were thrashed 7-2. Later that month Dean and Lawton played alongside each other for the very first time. Everton played Tottenham Hotspur in an FA Cup tie at White Hart Lane and lost 4-3 – Lawton scored one and Dean got the other two.

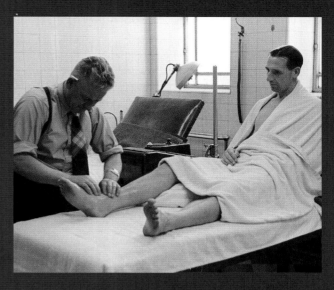

The following season saw Lawton replace Dean as the regular centre-forward in the Everton line-up and although the team finished in the bottom half of the table, Lawton's 28 goals made him the First Division's leading goalscorer.

In 1938-39, Everton won the title and once again Lawton was the top scorer in the division with 34 goals in 38 games, even though he was still a teenager.

It was just after his 19th birthday that he made his international debut, scoring for England in a 4-2 win against Wales in Cardiff. He became the youngest player to score on his England debut and he held that record until Marcus Rashford broke it in 2016.

Sadly, the outbreak of World War II totally disrupted Lawton's career and the chance to score more goals for Everton was gone. During the war, players could play for anyone and on Christmas Day 1940, Lawton played for Everton in the morning and Tranmere Rovers in the afternoon!

The games played during the war never counted in any official statistics and Tommy Lawton never scored another senior goal for Everton. When peace finally broke out in 1945 he left the club to join Chelsea.

His Everton career was short-lived but he will always be remembered as the boy who replaced Dixie Dean ... and did a very good job of doing so.

Mr. T. Kelly. (Secretary) Britton. Cunliffe. Sagar. Gee. Gillick. Mr. T. Cook. (Trainer)

Jackson. Geldard. Cook. Dean. Lawton. Stevenson. Dougall.

Watson. Jones. Mercer.

MY COUNTRY
FRANCE
by Djibril Sidibe

Here are some fun facts about my home country, France...

France is the largest country in the EU, and is known as 'the hexagon' because of its six-sided shape. It is known as l'hexagone.

France was the first country in the world to ban supermarkets from throwing away or destroying unsold food. Since February 2016, they must donate wastage to food banks or charities.

There is a law in France which prohibits people from calling their pigs Napoleon, after the famous French emperor.

Some of the great inventions were thought up by Frenchmen. The reading and writing system for the blind, braille, was developed by Louis Braille who was blinded as a child, physician René Laennec invented the stethoscope and Alexandre-Ferdinand Godefroy made the world's first hair dryer in 1888.

In 1830, Louis XIX was the King of France for just 20 minutes, the shortest ever reign! He took over from his father and immediately abdicated himself!

The world's oldest ever human was French! Jeanne Louise Calment was born on 21 February 1875 and died on 4 August 1997, aged 122. She lived through two World Wars and the invention of television, the modern motor car and aeroplanes! She was born three years before Everton Football Club was formed and died just after Howard Kendall had been appointed manager for the third time!!

Europe's highest mountain is in the French Alps - Mont Blanc is 4,810 metres high and takes between 10 to 12 hours to climb to the summit. Alternatively, you can take a leisurely 20-minute trip up on Europe's highest cable car.

Paris Gare du Nord is Europe's busiest railway station with some 190 million passengers passing through each year. Built in 1846, it is also one of the world's oldest stations.

The most successful club team in France is St Etienne, who have won the league ten times – although PSG have won six out of the last seven.

The world's greatest cycle race, the Tour de France, has been around for more than 100 years, with the first event held in 1903. Every July, cyclists race some 3,200km (2,000 miles) primarily around France in a series of stages over 23 days, with the fastest cyclist at each stage wearing the famous yellow jersey.

One of the most famous French monuments is the Eiffel Tower. It gets painted every seven years! There are 1,665 steps to the top.

AND SOME FACTS ABOUT ME...

- I was born in Troyes, a town in France, and signed for Troyes FC when I was 8-years-old.

- I was at LOSC Lille in 2014 when Everton played them in the Europa League. Idrissa Gueye was a team-mate.

- I signed for Monaco in 2016 and we won the league in my first season – the only time in the last seven years that PSG has not been champions of France.

- My first goal for France was against England in 2017.

- I was in the French squad that won the World Cup in 2018.

In-action against England

With my hands on the World Cup

EVERTON LADIES

WILLIE KIRK is the manager of Everton Ladies, who play in Women's Super League 1...

ENGLAND REACHING THE SEMI-FINAL OF THE WOMEN'S WORLD CUP MUST HAVE BEEN GREAT FOR THE GAME...

Well it was a very exciting tournament for a start and the best impact is that young girls can now have female football heroes. I think that's really important because they have never had that before as the female players were never really in the spotlight. The World Cup was watched by millions and millions of people and it was a real success.

AND OF COURSE ONE OF OUR FORMER PLAYERS, PHIL NEVILLE, IS IN CHARGE OF THE TEAM...

The appointment of Phil was one of the best moves the Football Association has ever made. The standards that he has brought into the international set-up are immense and he wants nothing but the best for his players. He was like that here at Everton when he was a player. And no other manager would have been able to get David Beckham to take his young daughter, Harper, to a game!

That gets shown all around the world and, again, young girls will see that and be inspired by it. If someone as massive as David Beckham is watching a game then many, many more will follow.

YOU BROUGHT IN SEVERAL NEW PLAYERS LAST SUMMER TO STRENGTHEN YOUR SQUAD...

We recruited six so there was a great feeling amongst our squad and there was a spring in our step anyway

following the World Cup. We brought in some great characters and girls with great experience at both club and international level. Tinja-Riikka Korpela, the goalkeeper, has over 80 international caps for Finland, she's played in the European Championships and has won the Bundesliga with Bayern Munich so she can play in any league in the world. Kika van Es has been the captain of Ajax, she has won the European Championship with Holland and finished runner-up in the World Cup final, so can she play in England? Of course she can.

THE EVERTON TEAM WILL PLAY AT WALTON HALL PARK THIS SEASON - HOW IMPORTANT WAS IT FOR YOU TO GET YOUR OWN GROUND?

Last season we had the lowest average attendance of all the teams in the top two divisions and for a club of Everton's size that is just wrong. Walton Hall Park is so important on a number of levels. We are in the local area, not far from Goodison Park, and it's a place we can call home so hopefully the fans will come and see us. It would be fantastic to see Blues fans at Walton Hall Park with girls' names and numbers on the back of their shirts.

THE WOMEN'S GAME GOING FULL-TIME PROFESSIONAL HAS REALLY BEEN A MASSIVE TURNING POINT HASN'T IT?

Realistically, any young girl wanting to play football can now think about being a footballer as a career and they've never been able to do that before. An 8-year-old boy has always been able to say "I want to be a footballer" but an 8-year-old girl has never been able to say the same thing. That's a great thing. It's a realistic ambition for a young girl to want to play for Everton when she grows up.

THE GIRLS TAKE IMMENSE PRIDE IN PLAYING FOR EVERTON DON'T THEY?

It means every bit as much to the women as it does to the men. Every player who plays in my team has huge pride in the royal blue jersey. We've got a couple of players who were Liverpool supporters but they just want to play for Everton now.

TALKING OF LIVERPOOL, IT WAS GREAT TO BEAT THEM LAST SEASON!

It was fantastic and one of our aims this season is to be the best team in this city. Before we start to think about being the best team in the north or even in the whole country, we want to be better than Liverpool.

GUESS THE BLUES!

Here are some pictures of Everton in action in the Premier League. You have to name the Everton player and also his opponent - and the clue is that every opposition player pictured here also played for Everton!

See how many you can get - and give yourself an extra point if you can name the team we are playing against in each picture.

EVERTON PLAYER:

_____

OPPONENT:

_____

TEAM:

_____

EVERTON PLAYER:

_____

OPPONENT:

_____

TEAM:

_____

EVERTON PLAYER:

_____

OPPONENT:

_____

TEAM:

_____

EVERTON PLAYER:

_____

OPPONENT:

_____

TEAM:

_____

EVERTON PLAYER:

_____

OPPONENT:

_____

TEAM:

_____

EVERTON PLAYER:

_____

OPPONENT:

_____

TEAM:

_____

7

EVERTON PLAYER:

_____

OPPONENT:

_____

TEAM:

_____

8

EVERTON PLAYER:

_____

OPPONENT:

_____

TEAM:

_____

9

EVERTON PLAYER:

_____

OPPONENT:

_____

TEAM:

_____

10

EVERTON PLAYER:

_____

OPPONENT:

_____

TEAM:

_____

11

EVERTON PLAYER:

_____

OPPONENT:

_____

TEAM:

_____

12

EVERTON PLAYER:

_____

OPPONENT:

_____

TEAM:

_____

SCORES!

TOTAL:

34-36 POINTS: PREMIER LEAGUE TITLE CONTENDER

30-33 POINTS: TOP FOUR FINISH

26-29 POINTS: EUROPA LEAGUE QUALIFICATION

20-25 POINTS: MID-TABLE

19 POINTS OR FEWER: WHOOPS... IT'S RELEGATION FOR YOU!

Answers on page 63

ALL TOGETHER

It's never too early to start being a

NOW...

Blue – as all these fab pics show!

BLUES LEGEND
PETER REID

Despite being born and bred in Liverpool, Peter Reid started his career as a professional footballer with Bolton Wanderers. He played alongside future Everton manager Sam Allardyce whilst at Burnden Park and in 1977 he was in the Bolton side that was narrowly beaten by Everton over two legs in the semi-final of the League Cup.

The following year he helped the team to promotion from the Second Division into the top flight and in 1981 he was linked with a big-money move to Everton that never happened because he broke his leg. He fought back bravely from the injury and twelve months later got his move to Goodison Park for the knockdown fee of just £60,000.

It was one of the best pieces of transfer business that Everton Football Club has ever done. Reid is acknowledged as being one of the key players in Everton transforming themselves from a struggling side into the finest in Europe in the mid-80s. His experience, his knowledge of the game and his powerful personality helped the younger players in the Everton dressing room.

Reid won the FA Cup in 1984 when Everton defeated Watford 2-0 in the final at Wembley and the following year he played 57 games in all competitions as the League Championship came back to Goodison Park for

the first time since 1970. He also played in the European Cup Winners' Cup final that season, which Everton won – beating the Austrian side Rapid Vienna 3-1 in the final in Rotterdam. Three days after that historic victory Everton were back at Wembley for another FA Cup final but they lost 1-0 to Manchester United. Reid was a central figure of the game's major talking point. He was fouled by United defender Kevin Moran who was controversially sent-off for the challenge. It was the first ever FA Cup final sending off but it didn't help Everton much!

1985/86 was a season of double disappointment for the Blues as they finished second in the league to Liverpool and also lost in the FA Cup final to our city rivals. It was a bitter pill to swallow and, unbelievably, both teams had to do an open-top bus tour of the city the next day. Only one Everton player refused to get on the bus. Yes, you've guessed it... Peter Reid!

He did, however, board the England plane to Mexico two weeks later for the 1986 World Cup, where he played a major role in helping England reach the quarter-finals, where they lost to a Diego Maradona-inspired Argentina.

Reid was back among the medals in 1987 when Everton regained the Championship and he stayed for another two years before leaving to join Queens Park Rangers.

He ended his playing career with spells at Manchester City, Southampton, Notts County and Bury. After hanging up his boots, he moved into management and had spells at Manchester

City, Sunderland, Leeds United, Coventry City and Plymouth Argyle, as well as managing the national team of Thailand.

But his heart remained at Goodison Park. In total, he played 235 games for Everton, scoring 13 goals, and he is quite rightly regarded as a club legend. In 2006 he was inducted into the club's official Hall of Fame when he was announced as that year's Everton Giant.

GETTING TO KNOW...
ALEX IWOBI

WHERE AND WHEN WERE YOU BORN?

I was born in Lagos, the capital city of Nigeria on 3 May 1996 and the family moved to England when I was four-years-old.

WHEN DID YOU FIRST JOIN ARSENAL?

When I was still in primary school. I made my first-team debut in 2015 when I was 19-years-old in a League Cup match against Sheffield Wednesday. We lost but I made my Premier League debut in the following game when I replaced Mesut Ozil against Swansea City.

WHEN DID YOU SCORE YOUR FIRST PROFESSIONAL GOAL?

I think you know that! It was against Everton at Goodison Park! It was my first start in the Premier League and I scored the second goal in a 2-0 win just before half-time. Sorry about that!

YOU WON AN FA CUP WINNERS MEDAL IN 2017 DIDN'T YOU?

Yes I did but unfortunately I was an unused substitute in the 2-1 win against Chelsea at Wembley. Theo Walcott was alongside me on the bench and he didn't get on either. But I did manage to play at Wembley a few months later in the FA Community Shield, again against Chelsea. I started the game and Arsenal eventually won on penalties. I didn't have to take one because I had been substituted in the second half.

YOU'RE AN INTERNATIONAL FOR NIGERIA BUT YOU PLAYED FOR ENGLAND AT YOUTH LEVEL?

Yes I did and I was in the England Under-16 team that won the Victory Shield in 2011. We played Scotland, Northern Ireland and Wales and I managed to score against the Scots in the win that clinched the shield for us. However I wanted to play for the country of my birth so I decided to play my international football for Nigeria.

WHEN DID YOU WIN YOUR FIRST CAP?

In October 2015 when Nigeria played DR Congo. The game was played in Belgium to make it easier for the European based players to get there. I was selected in the provisional Nigerian squad for the 2016 Olympic Games in Rio but didn't make the final cut. I did make the squad for the World Cup in Russia in 2018 but it was disappointing and we went out at the group stage. But we were in a tough group with Argentina, Croatia and Iceland. I played against Gylfi Sigurdsson when we beat Iceland!

YOU ALSO PLAYED IN THE 2019 AFRICA CUP OF NATIONS?

Yes I did. We reached the semi-final but lost to Algeria when Riyad Mahrez scored deep into stoppage time. That was a massive blow for us.

WAS IT AN EASY DECISION TO SIGN FOR EVERTON?

The offer was too attractive for me to turn down. The manager was telling me, 'There is a spot for you, we will take care of you'. Basically, all the things you want to hear as a player. I always had that 'youngster' tag at Arsenal, so hopefully with this move I am able to make a name for myself in the Premier League and create history with Everton. The manager has worked with Richarlison for a long while and made a name for him. Hopefully he can do the same for not just me but Moise Kean and a few others who came in too.

YOU ARE THE REF!

Imagine you're at Goodison watching the Blues and the referee gets injured in the warm up... and you are asked to take over from him!

THINK YOU COULD DO IT?

Well, test yourself first with these questions about the rules of the game...

1. How far from the goal-line is the penalty spot?

2. What does VAR stand for?

3. What two colour cards can referees use during a game?

4. How many yards away from the ball does the defensive wall have to be before a free-kick is taken?

5. How many players can stand in a defensive wall from a free-kick – five, six or as many as you like?

6. If a defender passes the ball back to his goalkeeper, is the keeper allowed to pick it up?

7. How much of the ball must cross the line for the referee to give a goal – half of it, three-quarters of it or all of it?

8. Can an attacking player be offside from a throw-in?

9. Are goalies allowed to take a throw-in?

10. Are all the pitches in the Premier League exactly the same size?

11. Can a player score a goal by shooting direct from the kick-off?

12. If a player taking a throw-in manages to find the net without anyone else touching the ball, is it a goal?

ANSWERS ON PAGE 63

SCHOOL EXAM

Test your footy knowledge and your maths at the same time! See if you can work out the answers to these questions and go top of the class if you get them all correct!

#				
1	RICHARLISON'S SHIRT NUMBER	+	THE NUMBER OF TEAMS IN THE PREMIER LEAGUE	=
2	LIONEL MESSI'S SHIRT NUMBER	✗	THE NUMBER OF GOALS IN A HAT-TRICK	=
3	EVERTON'S FINISHING PREMIER LEAGUE POSITION LAST SEASON	+	GYLFI SIGURDSSON'S SHIRT NUMBER	=
4	THE NUMBER OF TIMES ENGLAND HAVE WON THE WORLD CUP	+	THE NUMBER OF GOALS RAHEEM STERLING SCORED IN LAST SEASON'S FA CUP FINAL	=
5	MICHAEL KEANE'S SHIRT NUMBER	✗	THE NUMBER OF TEAMS THAT PLAY IN AN FA CUP QUARTER-FINAL	=
6	THE NUMBER OF TEAMS IN THE FOUR DIVISIONS IN ENGLAND	−	WAYNE ROONEY'S LAST SHIRT NUMBER FOR EVERTON	=
7	ANDRE GOMES' SHIRT NUMBER	+	THE NUMBER OF GOALS ARSENAL SCORED IN THEIR EUROPA LEAGUE FINAL WIN AGAINST CHELSEA LAST SEASON	=
8	THE NUMBER OF GOALS IN THE LAST WORLD CUP FINAL WHEN FRANCE BEAT CROATIA	✗	LEIGHTON BAINES' SHIRT NUMBER	=
9	THE YEAR EVERTON LAST WON THE FA CUP	−	THE YEAR EVERTON FOOTBALL CLUB WAS FORMED	=
10	TOM DAVIES' SHIRT NUMBER	−	THE NUMBER OF LETTERS IN DOMINIC CALVERT-LEWIN'S NAME!	=
11	THE NUMBER OF TEAMS MARCO SILVA HAS MANAGED IN THE PREMIER LEAGUE	✗	THEO WALCOTT'S SHIRT NUMBER	=
12	MOISE KEAN'S AGE WHEN HE SIGNED FOR EVERTON IN AUGUST 2019	−	YERRY MINA'S SHIRT NUMBER	=

ANSWERS ON PAGE 63

RICHARLISON

EVERTON UNDER-23s
DAVID UNSWORTH

Everton Under-23s won the Premier League 2 title last season for the second time in three years. They also won the Premier League Cup to become the first Under-23 side to do the double. Their coach is our former player DAVID UNSWORTH...

Nobody loves Everton more than you Unsy so how did you feel doing the double last season?

Relieved! And I was excited for the players. We all know that at our level it's not all about winning leagues, but we try and run our squad like a first-team. We prepare properly and that stands them in good stead for when they play senior football, either at Everton or somewhere else. It's great for the players' profiles to be seen as winners and champions and it gives them a winning mentality. And, of course, it was terrific to clinch the league title at Goodison Park and then win the Cup there as well.

At what stage of the season did you genuinely start to think that you could go on and win the league?

Good question! We started off okay and that always gives you a good platform, but I would say that when the new year started and we were still up there, I started to think about wining the league. Beating Liverpool at Anfield in March was a big, big result for us. Not just in terms of beating a top team but the performance level was very high and I knew that would kick us on for the rest of the season.

There's nothing better than seeing an Everton team win at Anfield!

Well that was the first time in the seven seasons that I have been Under-23s manager that we've even played there. The away derby has always been at their Academy or Tranmere or Chester. It was a magic night – the players loved it and quite rightly so.

I wish we could play all our games at the 'proper' stadiums, like we used to do in the old days when I was an Everton reserve player. The young boys get so much more benefit from playing in a Premier League stadium, even when there aren't that many fans inside it.

That night we beat Liverpool at Anfield there were a few thousand in the Kop and there was a good atmosphere.

Why do we send young players out on loan?

It's part of their development journey. We spend a lot of time as coaches discussing how we can improve our players and sending them out on loan is one way. We will only do so if we think the club is right for the boy and if the time is right.

We cover every single game for every player who is out on loan and if, for some reason, we can't physically get a member of staff at the game we have the technology to watch them here at Finch Farm. We have a piece of kit that has access to every single game in the Football League and when I sit down to watch it, I can type in our player's name and it will give me all his action clips so I don't have to sit through the whole 90 minutes.

Wow! How does that work?

No idea!!! But it's a brilliant piece of software.

What do you enjoy most about being the manager of the Under-23s?

I love the team winning, I love watching individuals play well and I love seeing our boys turning out for the first team. It's a wonderful role when you're trying to win things for Everton Football Club and you're helping young footballers fulfil their potential.

MY COUNTRY

 **BRAZIL**

by BERNARD...

Brazil is the largest country in South America... and the 5th largest in the world.

It is the longest country in the world!

Our official language is Portuguese.

Football is the most popular sport in my country – we have won the World Cup five times. Our most famous player of all time is Pele. His real name is Edson Arantes do Nascimanto and he scored more than 1,000 goals in his career.

Brazil has hosted the World Cup finals on two occasions. In 1950 we lost in the final to Uruguay and in 2014 we were beaten 7-1 by Germany in the semi-final.

Away from football our most famous sportsman was the Grand Prix driver Ayrton Senna, who won the Formula One World Championship.

Brazil is very busy and there are more than 2,500 airports in the country. Only the USA has more.

Brazil has been the world's largest coffee exporter for 150 years

CAFES DO BRASIL

Ayrton Senna is the most successful Brazlian Formula One driver of all time

Our favourite music is samba, which was developed in Brazil in the 1800s.

The country's motto is 'Ordem e Progresso', meaning 'order and progress'.

Brasilia, the country's capital, is very new compared to other capital cities around the world. They started building it in 1956 and it took just 41 months to finish.

Brazil has been the world's largest exporter of coffee for more than 150

The Amazon River flows through Brazil

The famous Christ The Redeemer statue looks down over Rio de Janeiro

Brasília is one of the newest capital cities in the world

Copacabana Beach

In a recent survey, the most popular surname in Brazil was 'Silva'... but the boss is from Portugal so it's nothing to do with him!

Our most famous monument is the statue of Christ the Redeemer in Rio de Janeiro. It weighs 635 tons and is 38 metres high.

The largest river in the world, the Amazon, runs through Brazil. In the wet season the Amazon can be an incredible thirty miles wide at some points!

Feijoada is the national dish of Brazil which is a stew of beans with beef and pork. A popular dessert is brigadeiros, which are chocolate fudge balls.

The Brazilian carnival, which takes place every year in Rio de Janeiro, attracts 2million people each day - making it the biggest street party in the world!

The most famous beach in Brazil is the Copacabana in Rio. In 1994 the world's largest ever concert attendance watched Rod Stewart perform on Copacabana beach - an amazing 3.5million!

FACTS ABOUT ME

- I was born in Belo Horizonte, the sixth largest city in Brazil. In 1950, USA beat England 1-0 in Belo Horizonte - one of the biggest shocks in World Cup history.

- I played in Brazil's 7-1 World Cup defeat to Germany in 2014 - also in Belo Horizonte.

- My full name is Bernard Anício Caldeira Duarte.

- My first team was Atletico Maneiro and my transfer to Shakhtar Donetsk is still the biggest fee the club has ever received.

- I won three Ukranian Premier League titles with Shakhtar before joining Everton.

The great Pele - Brazil's most famous footballer

The Rio Carnival is the biggest in the world

QUIZ ANSWERS

PAGE 9 - NEW KIT PHOTOSHOOT

1 B
2 B
3 A
4 C
5 A

PAGE 12-13 WAS IT A GOAL

1 Miss (Gylfi missed this penalty but scored from the rebound!)
2 Goal
3 Goal
4 Miss
5 Miss
6 Goal
7 Miss
8 Goal
9 Goal
10 Miss
11 Goal
12 Miss
13 Miss
14 Goal

PAGE 18-19 MICHAEL KEANE'S NAME THE STAR QUIZ

1 Aaron Wan-Bissaka (Manchester United)
2 Joe Gomez (Liverpool)
3 John Stones (Manchester City)
4 Erik Lamella (Tottenham Hotspur)
5 Pierre-Emerick Aubameyang (Arsenal)
6 Jack Grealish (Aston Villa)
7 Robert Snodgrass (West Ham)
8 Jonjo Shelvey (Newcastle United)
9 Diogo Jota (Wolves)
10 Phil Jagielka (Sheffield United)
11 Nathan Redmond (Southampton)
12 Jonny Evans (Leicester City)
13 Andro Townsend (Crystal Palace)
14 Shane Duffy (Brighton)

PAGE 23 SPOT THE BALL

B

PAGE 35 HOLY TRINITY FOREVER

1 David Beckham
2 Dixie Dean
3 Alex Ferguson
4 Bobby Moore
5 Alan Shearer
6 Dennis Bergkamp
7 Christiano Ronaldo
8 Tom Finney

PAGE 38 GROWN-UP QUIZ

1 Espen Baardsen
2 Paul Gerrard
3 Tim Howard
4 Jason Kearton
5 Nigel Martyn
6 Jan Mucha
7 Joel Robles
8 John Ruddy
9 Steve Simonsen
10 Maarten Stekelenburg
11 Iain Turner
12 Stefan Wessels
13 Sander Westerweld
14 Richard Wright